WITHDRAWN

Published by Creative Education
123 South Broad Street, Mankato, Minnesota 56001

Creative Education is an imprint of The Creative Company.
Design by Stephanie Blumenthal
Production design by The Design Lab
Art direction by Rita Marshall

Printed by Corporate Graphics in the United States of America

Photographs by Corbis (Brian Bailey, Blue Lantern Studio, Fine Art Photographic Library, Rob Howard, Hulton–Deutsch Collection, The Mariners' Museum, Owaki–Kulla)

Illustrations copyright © 2006 Etienne Delessert, © 1993 Guy Billout, © 1993 Gary Kelley, © 2004 John Thompson

Library of Congress Cataloging-in-Publication Data

Fandel, Jennifer.
Puns, allusions, and other word secrets / by Jennifer Fandel.
p. cm. — (Understanding poetry)
Includes index.
ISBN 978-1-58341-341-8
1. Poetics—Juvenile literature. 2. Puns and punning—Juvenile literature. 3. Allusions—Juvenile literature. I. Title. II. Understanding poetry (Mankato, Minn.)

PN1059.P86F36 2005
808.1—dc22   2004058229

CPSIA: 031010 PO1220

9 10 11 12

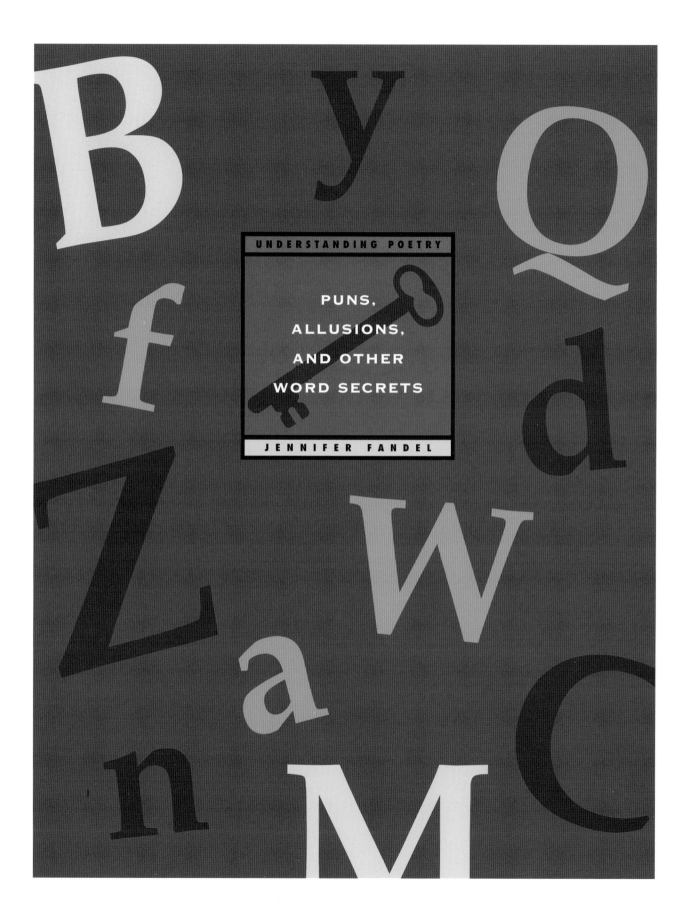

UNDERSTANDING POETRY

PUNS,
ALLUSIONS,
AND OTHER
WORD SECRETS

JENNIFER FANDEL

CREATIVE EDUCATION

Imagine a group of poets walking down the street. They trip on a crack in the sidewalk, and the contents of their bags and briefcases fly out. The word bumble zips by you. The word ache tumbles to the ground. And some crazy and unexpected phrases, such as a rocket of loneliness or flower-pot windowpane, get caught in the wind. Without words, poetry (and poets!) would not exist. Words create the images that make poems come alive. And the possibilities for words are endless. You can shade and color them with meanings. You can mold them, like clay, in different ways. You can put them in nearly any order. And when you listen closely, words contain an orchestra of sound.

Long ago, when kings and queens ruled much of Europe, poets entertained the royal courts and wrote poems for special occasions. These poets were usually selected because they could think fast on their feet, throwing out a quick line about a situation and poking fun at their enemies, much like today's stand-up comics. They were good at choosing words, whether for a laugh or to reflect on a solemn occasion, such as the wedding of a prince or the death of a court official. They were also educated people who had read the stories of the ancient Greeks and Romans, remembering key details they could use to make comparisons between the current king or queen and the most powerful or most beautiful rulers of ancient times. While most poets today aren't employed by royal courts, they continue to be admired for their ability with words.

Well-chosen words surprise readers and invite them into a poem's "secret world." Words can be full of mystery and magic every time you say them. They are full of beauty, meaning, and sound, and they can reveal new things about the world around you. Poets write to make these new discoveries, but they also write because of their love for words. Written on paper and shared with others, words have the power to stir our emotions and transport us to different places and times.

Sometimes you'll hear sportscasters say that a certain tennis move or baseball catch is "pure poetry" or poetry in motion. This means that the moment is beautiful, natural, and nearly perfect. These beautiful moves in poetry happen largely because of the words poets choose.

Why do poets choose the words they do when writing poems? And what do these words reveal to their readers? In **prose**, because writers have more time and space to get their point across, each word isn't as important as the overall meaning. But because poems often use few words, each word carries greater weight. Every word helps give the poem meaning.

Words can have many meanings, depending upon how they are used in a sentence. To better understand the meaning of words, you need to understand the difference between **literal** and **figurative** language. If you use a word literally, you are using the dictionary definition of the word to get your meaning across. If you use a word figuratively, you are presenting an image to get an idea across. For example, let's say that someone's eyes are brown. The descriptive word brown is used literally. It helps readers picture the color of the person's eyes. But let's change the phrase to "Her eyes are chocolate." We know that her eyes aren't really chocolate. We are using the word "chocolate" figuratively to explain what kind of brown her eyes are: the brown color of chocolate.

In addition, words can have certain **connotations**. In the example above, we might think of more than a color when we read "Her eyes are chocolate." When we hear the word "chocolate," we might imagine something that is sweet, rich, and very dark. When you read about a girl's eyes being chocolate, you'll probably imagine that she has dark brown eyes, but you may also imagine that her eyes show that she's a sweet, kind person. When thinking about word choices in your own poems, you need to be aware of the different meanings that your poem may reveal to readers. Sometimes exchanging your poems with other poets will help you find out if their interpretation of your words is different from your original meaning.

Let's look at the way Chilean poet Pablo Neruda (1904–73) has chosen his words in his poem "Poetry." In it, he describes the moment he fell in love with words and found the importance of poetry in his life.

POETRY

And it was at that age . . . Poetry arrived
in search of me. I don't know, I don't know where
it came from, from winter or a river.
I don't know how or when,
no, they were not voices, they were not
words, nor silence,
but from a street I was summoned,
from the branches of night,
abruptly from the others,
among violent fires
or returning alone,
there I was without a face
and it touched me.

I did not know what to say, my mouth
had no way
with names,
my eyes were blind,
and something started in my soul,
fever or forgotten wings,
and I made my own way,
deciphering
that fire,
and I wrote the first faint line,

faint, without substance, pure
nonsense,
pure wisdom
of someone who knows nothing,
and suddenly I saw
the heavens
unfastened
and open,
planets,
palpitating plantations,
shadow perforated,
riddled
with arrows, fire and flowers,
the winding night, the universe.

And I, infinitesimal being,
drunk with the great starry
void,
likeness, image of
mystery,
felt myself a pure part
of the abyss,
I wheeled with the stars,
my heart broke loose on the wind.

In this poem, Neruda uses a lot of figurative language to help readers feel the same joy that he felt as he discovered poetry. We know, for instance, that Neruda isn't being literal when he says that he did not have a face. Instead, he uses figurative language, making an image that helps readers feel as he did. What do you think Neruda means when he says he did not have a face? And what do you think some of his other figurative language means?

You probably also notice that Neruda uses a lot of words relating to nature and the planets. When you hear the words stars, night, and fire, what do they make you think of? Do the words have any connotations, or additional meanings, that you might bring into the poem as you read?

You have thousands of words at your fingertips when you write. Thinking about their different meanings can help you reveal new ideas in your poems, and it can also help you discover new possibilities as you write.

Poets make it their job to search for the perfect word. But some poets find that the perfect word doesn't yet exist, so they make up a word or use a real word in an uncommon way. American poet E. E. Cummings (1894–1962) made a career of making up words, combining words, and breaking words down so readers pay more attention to the sounds and meanings. Take a look at his poem "in Just-" and pay attention to the sounds of his words. Try to read the words exactly as they appear on the page. For the best effect, read this poem aloud.

IN JUST-

in Just-
spring   when the world is mud-
luscious the little
lame balloonman

whistles   far   and wee   from hop-scotch and jump-rope and

and eddieandbill come   it's
running from marbles and   spring
piracies and it's   and
spring   the

when the world is puddle-wonderful   goat-footed

the queer   balloonMan   whistles
old balloonman whistles   far
far   and   wee   and
and bettyandisbel come dancing   wee

11

Cummings makes some fantastic word combinations, such as mud-luscious and puddle-wonderful. Although we normally never hear these words together, they somehow make a lot of sense in the **context** of Cummings's poem. They also fill readers with surprise. Additionally, the poet combines names of people to form new, unexpected words such as bettyandisbel and balloonman. Why do you think he combined names like this? What effect do these combined names have on the poem?

Making up words or using words in an uncommon way can be a fun thing to do, and it may help you make new discoveries about language. Typically, poets say that nouns and verbs are the most important parts of a poem. Less important are the adjectives and adverbs, since they provide more information about the nouns and verbs. Least important are the other words: conjunctions, prepositions, and articles. While all of these parts of speech may be necessary to write a poem, poets always try to emphasize nouns and verbs. They challenge themselves to use one perfect word instead of many words that say the same thing. And if this means bending language to do new things, poets will do it.

A good example of bending language and using words in an uncommon way can be seen in "Kidnap Poem," by **contemporary** African-American poet Nikki Giovanni (1943–). This is another great poem to read aloud. Notice how the poet twists words to do exactly what she wants them to do.

KIDNAP POEM

ever been kidnapped
by a poet
if i were a poet
i'd kidnap you
put you in my phrases and meter
you to jones beach
or maybe coney island
or maybe just to my house
lyric you in lilacs
dash you into the beach
to complement my see
play the lyre for you
ode you with my love song
anything to win you
wrap you in the red Black green
show you off to mama
yeah if i were a poet i'd kid
nap you

Perhaps you noticed something a little strange in Giovanni's poem: She uses some nouns, such as meter and lyric, as verbs. In other words, she transforms subjects into actions. While this might sound difficult, it just requires thinking about words a little differently. When you read phrases such as "meter you" and "lyric you," what kinds of actions do you imagine? Do you think this was the best way for Giovanni to express her ideas? If Giovanni used regular verbs, do you think she could have expressed her ideas so quickly?

Of course, the most important part of playing with words is making sure that your ideas are understandable to your readers. Poems don't have to be puzzles, and they don't have to be hard to understand. In most cases, as long as you put your ideas in a clear context, your readers shouldn't have any problems understanding what you are trying to say. So go ahead. Play with words, trying different or unusual ways of expressing your ideas. You'll discover that the possibilities are endless!

People have always used words to make people laugh. When you started learning about the meanings of words as a child, you probably told knock-knock jokes and other jokes that used **puns**. Some of the most common jokes are puns. Most people, young and old alike, enjoy puns because they reveal how crazy and fun words can be.

Puns are often made when people use a word to mean two different things. Typically, puns work best with **homonyms**, such as hymn/him, pour /poor, and hair/hare.

Here's a pun that you may have heard before:

Question: What did one mushroom say to the other mushroom?

Answer: You're a fungi! ("A fun guy!")

People often groan when they hear puns, but that doesn't stop people from having fun with language. The English playwright and poet William Shakespeare (1564–1616) was a master at punning in his plays. For example, in the play *Romeo and Juliet*, a badly injured character says, "Ask me tomorrow and you shall find me a grave man." The word "grave" means "serious," but Shakespeare used it as a joke, since the man would be dead the next day. It may not sound like something to joke about, but Shakespeare made puns anywhere he could!

E. E. Cummings liked to play with the visual effects of words and made a series of visual word puns, including the untitled poem below. Visual word puns show readers a few different meanings within a word or phrase.

l(a

le
af
fa

ll
s)
one
l

iness

Try reading this visual pun by looking at what is inside the parentheses first. To make it easier, let's look at it horizontally: l(a leaf falls)oneliness. In Cummings's poem, he is trying to play with the image of a leaf falling and the feeling of loneliness. Why do you think he broke up the words the way he did? Do you see any other words within his visual poem that may help you understand the feeling he's talking about?

Some poets just like to play with language to get laughs from their readers. In the following poem, American poet John Ciardi (1916–86) gets readers' curiosity up with a really long title and delivers his punch line after it.

ON BEING MUCH BETTER THAN MOST AND YET NOT QUITE GOOD ENOUGH

There was a great swimmer named Jack
Who swam ten miles out—and nine back.

Other poets like to work with funny rhymes, sounds, and twists in language. One of the best-known American poets to do this was Ogden Nash (1902–71). Nash's poems were known by some readers as "Nashers," and people labeled his rhyming style

wrenched rhyme because he often forced words to rhyme

by using funny endings, mixing up the order of words, or using words in an unusual

way. He does this in his poem "The Duck."

THE DUCK

Behold the duck.
It does not cluck.
A cluck it lacks.
It quacks.
It is specially fond
Of a puddle or pond.
When it dines or sups,
It bottoms ups.

While readers often look to poetry to find out more about themselves and the world,

sometimes they just want to laugh and have fun. Playing with the meanings of words or

the words themselves can be a good time in itself. And making people laugh is one of the

best and most immediate rewards a poet can receive.

Poets also choose words for the larger significance they may have. These special words are known as **allusions** and **symbols**. Allusions allow you to refer to something or someone without actually saying who or what you are talking about. Nonetheless, the meaning should still be clear. In many ways, allusions are easy to understand for those who also experienced the same thing the poet did. The generation that lived through the attacks on the World Trade Center and the Pentagon on September 11, 2001, will always understand the allusion when the towers fell. This allusion to the attacks might not immediately make sense to people 100 years from now, though, and it might not make sense to people in other countries who didn't see or hear about the event.

We can see a good example of an allusion in the following two stanzas of the poem "When Lilacs Last in the Dooryard Bloom'd," by American poet Walt Whitman (1819–92).

1

When lilacs last in the dooryard bloom'd,

And the great star early droop'd in the western sky in the night,

I mourn'd, and yet shall mourn with ever-returning spring.

Ever-returning spring, trinity sure to me you bring,

Lilac blooming perennial and drooping star in the west,

And thought of him I love.

6

Coffin that passes through lanes and streets,

Through day and night with the great cloud darkening the land,

With the pomp of the inloop'd flags with the cities draped in black,

With the show of the States themselves as of crape-veil'd women standing,

With processions long and winding and the flambeaus of the night,

With the countless torches lit, with the silent sea of faces and the unbared heads,

With the waiting depot, the arriving coffin, and the sombre faces,

With dirges through the night, with the thousand voices rising strong and solemn,

With all the mournful voices of the dirges pour'd around the coffin,

The dim-lit churches and the shuddering organs—where amid these you journey,

With the tolling tolling bells' perpetual clang,

Here, coffin that slowly passes,

I give you my sprig of lilac.

This poem is about the death of U.S. president Abraham Lincoln. Whitman never says anything directly about Lincoln; he uses allusions. He talks about the casket making a journey through towns. For the people who lived through this event, this image would remind them of how Lincoln's casket traveled through many cities and towns on its way to the burial ground in Illinois, Lincoln's home state. For the people mourning Lincoln's death, Whitman's poem spoke to them. However, this doesn't mean that Whitman's poem has only one meaning. While Whitman wrote it to speak about the death of Lincoln specifically, the poem also speaks in general about losing a leader or a figure of strength. If you picked up the poem today, not knowing anything about it, you probably wouldn't think, "I'll bet this is about Lincoln." Instead, you'd understand the overall feeling that Whitman expressed through the poem.

DO NOT GO GENTLE INTO THAT GOOD NIGHT

Do not go gentle into that good night,
Old age should burn and rave at close of day;
Rage, rage against the dying of the light.

Though wise men at their end know dark is right,
Because their words had forked no lightning they
Do not go gentle into that good night.

Good men, the last wave by, crying how bright
Their frail deeds might have danced in a green bay,
Rage, rage against the dying of the light.

Wild men who caught and sang the sun in flight,
And learn, too late, they grieved it on its way,
Do not go gentle into that good night.

Grave men, near death, who see with blinding sight
Blind eyes could blaze like meteors and be gay,
Rage, rage against the dying of the light.

And you, my father, there on the sad height,
Curse, bless, me now with your fierce tears, I pray.
Do not go gentle into that good night.
Rage, rage against the dying of the light.

Commonly seen in poems, symbols are words that represent an idea. Typically, people understand the meaning of a symbol based on common stories, myths, things that they have read, or ideas commonly associated with that word. For example, because we typically wake up when the sun rises, we often think of light as representing wakefulness or life. And because we often sleep when the sun sets, we typically think of darkness as something meaning rest or death. You can see how the two symbols night and light work in the poem "Do Not Go Gentle into That Good Night," by Welsh poet Dylan Thomas (1914–53).

When you read this poem, the emotions in it tell you that Thomas is talking about something much bigger than "night" and "light." He uses these symbols to talk about his father's coming death. How do Thomas's symbols affect you as you read? Do his ideas about life and death come through clearly? And why do you think Thomas used these symbols instead of speaking directly about death and life?

In many respects, allusions and symbols are short, easy ways of conveying a bigger idea. Instead of explaining what something means, you can simply use a word or phrase to present the idea for you. This is one area of word choice that isn't dependent upon coming up with new and surprising words. It's important, though, to pick words that make your allusions and symbols understandable and clear.

Poems can be told from many different angles, or perspectives.

Point of view is a significant device used in poems. (It is also important in short stories and novels.) A poet can use first-person point of view (I, we), second-person (you), or third-person (he, she, it, they) in a poem. Point of view greatly affects how the audience understands the poem.

If a poet uses the word I, readers might guess that the poet is sharing his or her personal ideas. Additionally, "I" can represent the speaker of the poem. Just because the poet wrote the poem using "I" doesn't mean that the experiences and feelings of the poem are actually true things that happened to the poet. They may be, but the poet could just be imagining things, too. A poet could also be stepping into someone else's experience, real or imagined, and talking from his or her point of view. This is called a **dramatic monologue**.

The poem "Hanging Fire," by American poet Audre Lorde (1934–92), presents the feelings of a 14-year-old girl. This poem is a dramatic monologue, meaning that Lorde stepped inside the girl's shoes in order to tell the story as the girl might see it.

HANGING FIRE

I am fourteen
and my skin has betrayed me
the boy I cannot live without
still sucks his thumb
in secret
how come my knees are
always so ashy
what if I die
before morning
and momma's in the bedroom
with the door closed.

I have to learn how to dance
in time for the next party
my room is too small for me
suppose I die before graduation
they will sing sad melodies
but finally
tell the truth about me

There is nothing I want to do
and too much
that has to be done
and momma's in the bedroom
with the door closed.

Nobody even stops to think
about my side of it
I should have been on Math Team
my marks were better than his
why do I have to be
the one
wearing braces
I have nothing to wear tomorrow
will I live long enough
to grow up
and momma's in the bedroom
with the door closed.

Hearing this story of the girl from her perspective helps us understand how the details of her life are very real and important to her. If Lorde had told the story by simply talking *about* the girl, we would lose the special way the girl talks and the way in which she presents the insights and concerns of her particular world.

Poems can also use second-person point of view. As with first-person, there are a few different uses of you. Sometimes poets use "you" to talk to themselves, almost as if they are speaking to themselves in a mirror. If, for example, you were writing a poem about waking up late, you might begin "It happened the day you woke up late. . . ." The most common use of "you" is when speaking directly to someone or something. This can be seen in personal poems of love or friendship, or more public poems such as "blessing the boats," by contemporary African-American poet Lucille Clifton (1936–).

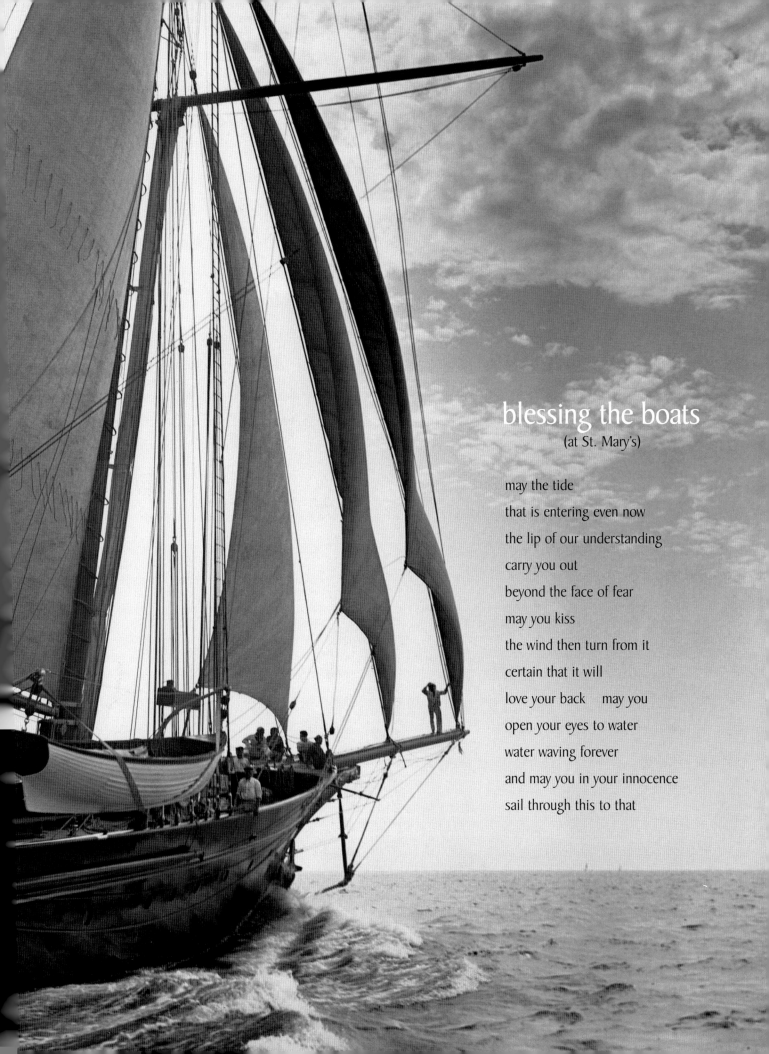

blessing the boats

(at St. Mary's)

may the tide

that is entering even now

the lip of our understanding

carry you out

beyond the face of fear

may you kiss

the wind then turn from it

certain that it will

love your back   may you

open your eyes to water

water waving forever

and may you in your innocence

sail through this to that

Clifton, in her poem, addresses the boats with a blessing. Using words such as "may you," Clifton makes her wishes for the boats clear. Additionally, it's easy for readers to apply this information to their own lives. Hearing or reading the word "you" makes us feel that Clifton is also speaking to us. As a result, reading Clifton's blessing of the boats is like reading a blessing for our own lives.

Finally, there's third-person point of view (she, he, it, they). If you use third-person, you look at the subject in a more **objective** way. You report what you see without mentioning yourself (I) or the audience (you). This point of view is helpful when you simply want to show something without making readers aware of the writer or the audience. In this way, it's similar to a newspaper report.

Let's look at how different points of view change our understanding of the first line of Lorde's poem "Hanging Fire." The line in first-person reads: "I am fourteen and my skin has betrayed me." We get a sense of the girl's feelings and beliefs with the use of "I." This changes, however, with the use of second-person: "You are fourteen and your skin has betrayed you." Hearing "you," we might apply the details to ourselves. The use of third-person gives us a whole new perspective: "She is fourteen and her skin has betrayed her." In this version, we are removed from the feelings of the girl. Instead, the line reads more like a judgment about the girl.

You have a lot of options when it comes to point of view in poems. You may find that some poems seem to fit better with a certain point of view. Experimenting with perspective can drastically transform your poem and give readers an entirely different view of your subject.

The words that a poet chooses can help readers determine the voice and attitude of the poem. When poets talk about "voice," they are usually referring to characteristics in poems that help us learn more about a poet or the speaker of the poem. Sometimes we can figure out a person's personality, background, and beliefs simply by paying attention to the poet's word choices.

We can clearly hear the poet's voice in "This Is Just to Say," a poem by American poet William Carlos Williams (1883–1963).

THIS IS JUST TO SAY

I have eaten
the plums
that were in
the icebox

and which
you were probably
saving
for breakfast

Forgive me
they were delicious
so sweet
and so cold

In Williams's poem, the poet speaks casually, as if to his wife or good friend. It's easy to imagine this poem stuck on the refrigerator as a note; that's how casual and personal it is. Even though Williams is writing an apology, do you think he sounds genuinely sorry for eating the plums? Or do you think the poet is showing his sense of humor? How would you have felt to see this note left on your refrigerator by a friend or someone else you love?

The voice of a poem can also be expressed through the use of **slang** and **colloquialisms**. These types of word choices may help the poet present a subject realistically, especially when trying to portray the way people really speak. Slang and colloquialisms might also show a close relationship, since people often use casual word choices when communicating with other people they know well.

We can see an example of colloquial language in the poem "Mother to Son," by Langston Hughes (1902–67). Hughes, an African-American poet who began writing in the 1920s, thought it was important to use the language of poor and working-class African-Americans to make his poetry truer to the black experience.

MOTHER TO SON

Well, son, I'll tell you:
Life for me ain't been no crystal stair.
It's had tacks in it,
And splinters,
And boards torn up,
And places with no carpet on the floor—
Bare.
But all the time
I'se been a-climbin' on,
And reachin' landin's,
And turnin' corners,
And sometimes goin' in the dark
Where there ain't been no light.
So boy, don't you turn back.
Don't you set down on the steps
'Cause you finds it's kinder hard.
Don't you fall now—
For I'se still goin', honey,
I'se still climbin',
And life for me ain't been no crystal stair.

Hughes uses colloquial words such as $ain't$. He also uses shortened forms of words, such as $goin'$ and $kinder$ (for "kind of"). What effect does this have on you? Can you imagine the speaker of the poem when you hear this particular voice? Even though the speaker talks about hard times, she is trying to inspire her son to try hard and not get discouraged. Hughes chooses to repeat the word $don't$ frequently to emphasize the speaker's forceful and inspirational voice. Do you see other word choices that convey the optimistic voice of the poem?

Voice and attitude also come through loud and strong in the poem "Snow White and the Seven Dwarfs," by American poet Anne Sexton (1928–74). In her poetry collection *Transformations*, Sexton rewrote many of the Grimm Brothers' fairy tales by using "hip," modern word choices that convey her attitude toward the subjects. Pay attention to the effect these words have on the story in the excerpt on page 41.

Looking glass upon the wall . . .
The mirror told
and so the queen dressed herself in rags
and went out like a peddler to trap Snow White.
She went across seven mountains.
She came to the dwarf house
and Snow White opened the door
and bought a bit of lacing.
The queen fastened it tightly
around her bodice,
as tight as an Ace bandage,
so tight that Snow White swooned.
She lay on the floor, a plucked daisy.
When the dwarfs came home they undid the lace
and she revived miraculously.
She was as full of life as soda pop.
Beware of your stepmother,
they said.
She will try once more.

. . . Snow White, the dumb bunny,
opened the door
and she bit into a poison apple
and fell down for the final time.
When the dwarfs returned
they undid her bodice,
they looked for a comb,
but it did no good.
Though they washed her with wine
and rubbed her with butter
it was to no avail.
She lay as still as a gold piece.

Sexton's use of modern words such as Ace bandage and soda pop give the poem a modern feeling that you don't get when you read the original Grimm fairy tale. The speaker also doesn't hide some of her own attitudes in the poem when she refers to Snow White as a dumb bunny. So, do these word choices make you think of Snow White differently? How do these word choices make you feel as you read?

Word choice is extremely important in poetry because each word can alter the emotions in a poem. There is a general rule, though, that most poets recommend. Usually, simple word choices are the best. Beginning poets often think they need to use "poetic" words: words they wouldn't use in their everyday lives. The best word choices often come from your personal vocabulary. Because these words are natural to you, they will help you express your ideas honestly, from your own unique perspective, and that's what counts most when writing poetry. The key is to play, explore, and find out all that words can do.

1. Recommended Resources: Books. When searching for the perfect word, it's always a good idea to have a dictionary and thesaurus handy. Also check out the *Random House Word Menu* at your local library. It lets you search for words and their meanings by subject area. If you want to write a poem about cowboys, for example, this source helps you find all the appropriate words.

2. Activity: Word journal. Poets can never have enough words stored up for those times when their thoughts run dry. To make sure you have good ones at your fingertips, start keeping a journal of your favorites. Try to combine these words in uncommon ways, making new words and interesting phrases.

3. Activity: Changing points of view. Write a poem about your day using first-person point of view (I). After finishing this poem, write another version of the poem using second-person (you). Finally, write one more version using third-person (he or she). What is the effect of using each different point of view? Which poem do you like best?

4. Group Activity: A laugh-off. Gather a group of friends together and have each person write a humorous poem using at least two of the following: a pun, a long title, nonsense words, or a "wrenched rhyme" (words forced to rhyme). To see how effective your humorous poems are, hold a laugh-off by reading your poems in front of one another.

5. Activity: Note poem. Write an imitation of William Carlos Williams's poem "This Is Just to Say." Your poem should try to apologize to someone (the "you" in the poem) for something. But, like Williams's poem, your poem doesn't have to be completely serious or extremely sorry. Let your personality and feelings about the incident come through.

6. Activity: "Found words" poem. You can have a lot of fun with words by taking them out of their original context and mixing them up. To write a "found words" poem, cut interesting phrases and words out of newspapers and magazines. Once you have 10 to 20 words and phrases cut out, arrange the pieces to make a poem.

7. Activity: Personal symbols. Make a list of objects in your life and their hidden meanings. For example, a childhood teddy bear might represent security, while a bicycle may represent freedom. These objects are your personal symbols. Write a poem using a few symbols from this list. Then ask someone to read your poem and interpret your symbols.

8. Activity: Dramatic monologue. Step inside the mind of someone famous, someone with an interesting job, or someone, such as a parent or schoolmate, whom you just don't understand. Now, write a poem pretending that you are that person, using first-person point of view (I). Try to discover new things about the person by speaking with his or her voice.

9. Activity: Rewriting fairy tales. Choose a common fairy tale, such as "Hansel and Gretel" or "Cinderella," and rewrite the story in poetic form using slang and colloquial language. Try to bring out your attitude about the characters. Do you think Hansel and Gretel are too greedy? Do you think Cinderella is too nice to her wicked stepsisters? Tell the story as you think it might be told today.

10. Activity: Backwards poetry. If a poem is giving you trouble, try rewriting it backwards. Put your last line at the top and your first line at the bottom. Or, to mix it up a little more, put your last word at the top and your first word at the bottom. In any case, this should help you see new word combinations and unnecessary words.

Glossary

allusions: words that refer to a subject without making the subject clearly known

colloquialisms: informal words used in casual conversation

connotations: additional meanings associated with words

contemporary: of the present time

context: the information around a word that helps give it a specific meaning

dramatic monologue: a type of poem that consists of a person speaking about his or her life using first-person point of view (I)

figurative: relating to language that describes a subject but does not define it literally

homonyms: words that sound the same but are spelled differently and have different meanings, such as bear and bare or eye and I

literal: relating to something actual or factual

objective: involving facts rather than emotions; the opposite of subjective

point of view: the perspective used when telling a story or writing a poem

prose: writing that is composed in paragraphs rather than stanzas; short stories and essays are types of prose

puns: jokes made from word play, such as words that sound the same and mean different things

slang: colorful words and phrases made popular during certain time periods or within certain groups of people

symbols: words or images that represent something else

SELECTED WORKS

Ciardi, John. *The Hopeful Trout and Other Limericks.* New York: Houghton Mifflin, 1991.

Cummings, E. E. *Selected Poems.* New York: Liveright Publishing, 1994.

Giovanni, Nikki. *The Collected Poetry of Nikki Giovanni: 1968–1998.* New York: HarperCollins, 2003.

Hughes, Langston. *The Collected Poems of Langston Hughes.* New York: Knopf, 1995.

Lorde, Audre. *Collected Poems of Audre Lorde.* New York: Norton, 2000.

Nash, Ogden. *The Pocket Book of Odgen Nash.* New York: Simon and Schuster, 1991.

Thomas, Dylan. *Selected Poems, 1934 to 1952.* New York: New Directions, 2003.

Whitman, Walt. *Poems: Walt Whitman* (Everyman's Library Pocket Poets). New York: Knopf, 1994.

Williams, William Carlos. *Selected Poems.* New York: New Directions, 1985.

INDEX